One Wren's War

Margaret Munday-Whitaker's life during the
Second World War on the Isle of Wight
as told to

Irene Burkett

BOOKS

Designed and produced by
K. Wheeler and Pressready Artwork
© 2012
pressreadyartwork@onwight.net

Published by
KSW Books
Part of Pressready Artwork

Distributed by Irene Burkett
ireneburkett@hotmail.com

ISBN 978 0 9574540 0 2

Printed in England by
Bishops Printers
bishops.co.uk

Foreword

During the Second World War the Isle of Wight played a strategic and very important role in deterring German forces from reaching the mainland of England. It's geographical position meant that any successful invasion of the Island would be of enormous advantage in reaching Portsmouth or Southampton both of which were primary shipping ports and an important part of the Naval Defences of England.

The Isle of Wight took many hits from German bombers trying to destroy it's operational bases and many air raids were suffered by Islanders. V1 and V2 bombs (commonly known as doodlebugs), explosive bombs and landmines, all became part of Island life.

During the bombardment many men, women and children were killed and injured and nearly 11,000 buildings were destroyed.

Throughout 1942, 17,000 service personnel, plus Homeguard, were deployed in different parts of the Island and the coastal gun batteries were continually guarded from 1939.

This book is dedicated to Margaret Munday-Whitaker and her fellow Wrens on the Isle of Wight in World War Two and to all the inspirational women who successfully stepped into jobs that their men had previously occupied.

They combined family and working life as though it was something they had always been used to.

Margaret will say, "Well we just got on with it", and they did. We owe them all a huge vote of thanks for their selfless actions in keeping the country running. This they did with dedication and humour.

Christobel Pankhurst, of the Suffragette Movement, wrote: "It is our duty to make this world a better place for women." And "Ability is sexless." Christobel would have been proud of these women who were trailblazers in their own right.

For my son and daughter in law, Richard and Jackie Burkett who have embarked on their own new adventure in New Zealand

I Join the Wrens

It was 1941 and I was so excited. At last I was a Wren, me, Margaret Munday-Whitaker. I had applied at age 16 but had not been successful because I was still young and had not yet acquired skills relevant to the work of the Wrens. After my first interview I had decided to train in accountancy and so desperately wanted to be accepted into the Senior Service. Now at 18 years old I was to be part of the Women's Royal Naval Services. I had wanted to be a Wren for so long and now my dream had come true.

Living with my granny on the Isle of Wight, although I had been prepared to go almost anywhere, I was lucky to be posted locally. The Island is small and very beautiful and situated just off the coast of Portsmouth. Because it was so important to the success of the war effort geographically I also felt very proud playing my part in the success of the war. There could be no more important role for me at this time.

I had been a volunteer at the civilian telephone exchange since turning 16 years of age. My hours were from nine o'clock in the morning to nine o'clock at night. This was how my Sundays were spent.

The exchange was on the same site, in Puckpool Park, Ryde, as my later posting as a Wren. It was to become the Medina Naval establishment.

The telephone exchange was situated in one of the many underground tunnels that were adapted at Puckpool Fort to ensure that communication lines were kept open.

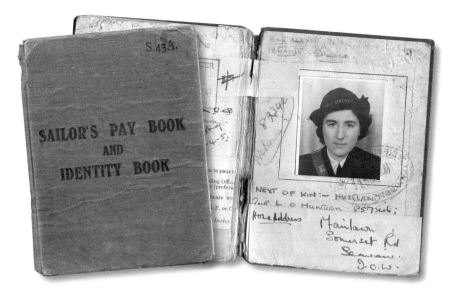

Margaret's pay book as a Wren. It carefully itemised her pay. She is proudly pictured in her uniform.

I felt very grown up looking around my new working environment, nearly two years later, and very proud of being in my navy blue, very smart, Wrens' uniform.

My posting was on *HMS Medina*, Fleet Air Arm, a land based fleet. Puckpool Park was a beautiful part of Ryde. Because I lived on the Island I was allowed to work on base and could continue to live with granny. I was pleased about this as my granny lived alone. It also saved money for the Navy. My job was to be in the Paymaster's office where my newly acquired accountancy skills could be used to the full.

The Isle of Wight was a very significant and strategic spot for the war effort, placed as it was between France and the mainland of England. It was, not surprisingly therefore, a regular target for German bombers. Both in Puckpool and Seaview, where my home with granny was, machine guns

2

were ready to shoot down the bombers which flew regularly over the Island.

My very first personal experience of the bombing had been at Seaview, in 1939, and a considerable time before I became a Wren.

It was bedtime and I was in the bathroom listening to the sounds of the Ack-Ack (Anti-Aircraft) guns. There was suddenly an almighty crash and rushing back into the bedroom I saw the ceiling collapse onto my bed. Moments later and I would have been in the bed. It was a very frightening experience and a very lucky escape indeed! The vibration of the guns had caused the damage.

That was to be the first of many of my frightening experiences and near fatal incidents as the war progressed.

I used to cycle to the base every day and always felt excited and privileged to be doing my part in the war effort. I helped to administer the payroll for the Wrens based on the Island. I assisted a Senior Wren but later on was promoted and became a Leading Wren who eventually taught other Wrens.

It was exciting to be meeting new friends from all over the British Isles and Ireland. I had so much more freedom now than ever before and was truly an adult now.

I had always had housework tasks set by granny as I was growing up and these had to be done every Saturday without fail and before anything else. One of the jobs was to polish the silver.

My lovely gran was a woman who had grown up in the Victorian era and she had a very strong work ethic. She taught me a lot over the years.

A post-war picture of Medina headquarters, now a thriving café in Puckpool Park, Ryde.

Granny was very short with a double chin, white hair and very rosy cheeks. She was plump and also a very good cook and was originally from Somerset, although my grandfather was an Islander and grew up on the Isle of Wight.

As the oldest in my family I had been sent to the Island to live and to keep grandmother company. Although I missed my brothers and sisters I always enjoyed Island life and now I was a Wren!

Becoming a Wren was much more exciting and a new chapter in my life. I was so very happy knowing too that the Isle of Wight was very important to the success of the war effort. This was also a time when women were being called upon to work in many of the important jobs that industry required. They were taking the place of the men who were now soldiers and heavily involved in fighting the war.

It was a time of great change all over the country and I was in the thick of it. This was particularly so for women. On the Isle of Wight they were taking jobs in the boat building industry, traditionally only men did these jobs.

They also became part of the huge numbers of women in the Land Army, literally an army of women sent to farms all over the country to keep them running and to ensure there were enough crops and farm animals available to feed the population of our country.

Manufacturing boats was very much an Island occupation for many and this was crucial to the success of the war. As I look back now, I realise that I was very much one of the forerunners in what was to change women's roles in society forever.

The interview to become a Wren was a tough one and I was asked many searching questions before my recruitment to the Senior Service was successful. Apart from the skills they already had, in my case it was accountancy, Wrens went straight into their jobs without benefit of any other training. There was no time for induction. The war could not wait so training was very much acquired on the job.

I worked with a Senior Wren, as with my accounting skills I was assigned to do the payroll. Everything had to be done in duplicate and we worked on two great bulky ledgers. It makes me smile when I think of them now and the difference today where everything is computerised.

Many of the Wrens were based on the cliffs at Culver Down at Bembridge. They lived in cottages and were the radio operators who were able to relay important and sensitive information, in Morse code, to the ships in the Channel. Subsequently they too were a frequent target for the German bombers.

There was a large communications centre close by. It was the

Culver Signal Station and was the first of a series of wireless stations built along the south coast by the Marconi Company for the Admiralty. The building was pulled down later and the site is now the car park of the Culver Haven Restaurant. The boundary stones still survive at each corner of the car park. There is also a commemorative plaque to remind us that the signal station was once there.

A delightful picture of the young Margaret, aged 21, in 1944.

I would often go up to Culver, with the Paymaster, to distribute the wages. My own wage was £3 per week, paid every two weeks. It seemed like a small fortune then as I had never had money of my own before.

CHAPTER TWO

Air Raids

My second experience of the devastating effects of the bombs was a very upsetting one. I had learned my skills in accountancy by training with a lady, Mrs Williams, who lived in Monkton Street in Ryde. Her husband, Mr Williams, was one of the teachers who taught at one of the local schools. I had been taught at the same school myself.

Sadly their house took a direct hit from one of the German bombs and they were killed. Their father had taken shelter in the cupboard under the stairs. The cupboard was amazingly the only thing left of the house and the old man miraculously survived. The rest of the house was totally demolished. He had come from London to escape the bombing there.

Both Mr and Mrs Williams were killed outright by the explosion. It had been Mrs Williams' birthday that day and celebrations had been held in the office earlier in the day. Tragically she was killed later that night. It was very sad and for me too, we had become good friends during the time that I had done my training and was very fond of her. Mr Williams was also greatly missed at his school, he had been a very popular teacher.

For all of the horror of such happenings, there were much lighter moments, sometimes even funny.

One such very funny incident was when the pay parade was in full swing. It happened every two weeks. On one of the occasions when the Pay Commander was giving out the Naval personnel's pay at Puckpool Park, all the men were on the veranda waiting to receive their pay. The parade was very formal and as the Paymaster reached each man, they had to take off their caps and he placed their wages, in cash, in each man's cap.

During one such pay parade there was an air raid and the Pay Commander was in the middle of the line with at least half of the men still to be paid. Everyone waited for the command to take cover. We were asked if we wanted to shelter but as pay was in progress we felt we ought to be brave and remain on parade. The men had no choice but to remain in line and the parade continued. Suddenly there were machine-gun bullets from a German bomber flying all around us. One bullet went right past the Commander's head and embedded itself in the wall behind. He carried on with the pay parade, quite unperturbed, and astonishingly, there were no injuries. The bullets stayed embedded there for many years.

On another occasion I was cycling down one of the hills in Seaview and as I did so yet another German bomber was flying low and machine-gunning everything in sight. There was nowhere to go and although absolutely terrified, I had no choice but to continue cycling. Bullets were flying all around me and a number of them hit one of the garden walls. For years afterwards those bullets remained until the wall was eventually replaced. I was very thankful that I escaped unhurt. Yet another miraculous escape!

My granny, not to be left out of the war effort, was determined to do her bit to help. She decided that her contribution would be to do the Wren's laundry. Every week the washing was done and I had to take the clean items back to the other girls.

I usually did so by putting the clean washing into a small, brown suitcase which I then tied onto my cycle. The Wrens

Wrens pictured on the seafront at Ryde. A water pipe runs along the kerb behind them for dealing with fires. Margaret is second from the right.

were billeted in Ryde and as the laundry was done in Seaview, I had approximately four miles to cycle. The suitcase was quite rigid, so not ideal to be perched on my cycle, especially when the journey was quite hilly.

I had set off to deliver the clean clothes and was cycling down a particularly steep hill, in Seaview, passing some soldiers who whistled at me as I flew by. The army had taken over a number of unoccupied houses to billet the soldiers in readiness for the Second Front so there was always a military presence on this road.

As I cycled past the soldiers the suitcase fell off the bike and hit the road with such force that it flew open and the clothes went everywhere. Since the laundry, on this occasion, had been mostly underwear there were bras and panties and the most embarrassing of all a pair of long black silk bloomers which when worn reached to the knees. The soldiers rushed to pick up the undergarments, holding them high and waving in the air as they did so and whistling all over again.

They had a glorious time but I was mortified and quickly put them all back in the suitcase which I tied back on my bike as fast as I could and then sped off with a very red face. It was three weeks before I could bring myself to take the same route. I was so completely embarrassed to face the soldiers again.

The Wrens at Ryde had to do fire watch at night and they each took shifts. One night I was on duty with one of the other Wrens. We were supposed to stay awake all night and be very vigilant and if there was an air raid to wake everyone up. On this particular night we all fell asleep and slept right through an air raid! We were lucky not to receive a good telling off from the Chief Wren, it could have been much worse but luckily for us it was kept quiet and we got away with it. We did not do that again.

The stores were at Puckpool and for the Wrens the first issue of clothing was free. After that we had to pay for whatever we wanted. One of my friends was a little Welsh Wren who rode the most enormous motor bike as a dispatch rider. One day she went to the stores and asked for some 'coms' The Petty Officer said, "We don't have coms." "Yes you do" she responded, "I have had them before"

The argument got quite heated with both sides convinced they were right. The Petty Officer, losing patience said, "You go get them yourself then." She did not need to be told twice and went straight to where the combs were kept and took two

Margaret looking splendid in her uniform with other colleagues serving with HMS Medina. Margaret is pictured second from right, on the second row.

of them. The Petty Officer looked very red faced. Because of her very broad Welsh accent he had thought she was saying 'coms' meaning 'combinations', those very warm, all in one undergarments which covered the body from the neck to just above the knees.

For all of the darker moments of the war, there were so many other moments, both funny and sad which brought people together and forged lasting friendships.

CHAPTER THREE

My Wedding

In 1942 I married my sweetheart, Leonard Munday whom I had known since I was 17. We met on Culver Down as we were both dog walking. He was in Coastal Defence, a gunner in the Royal Artillery. We had also met whilst cycling along the sea wall at Seaview. He was very shy and his friend introduced him to me. He was a very keen musician and played the saxophone and the clarinet and I had seen him playing with other musicians at one of the Vicarage garden parties

We enjoyed talking to each other and then started to go out together, sometimes to the Commodore cinema in Ryde or to the organised dances. The Services tried hard to give us all some leisure activities which certainly took our minds off the bombings which were constantly taking place.

We had got engaged in 1941. My fiancé had bought me a diamond engagement ring. Sadly three weeks later whilst gardening at granny's house in Seaview, I lost my beautiful ring. My lovely fiancé bought me a new ring, this time a twist design, with even more diamonds! The original was never found and later on the earth was concreted over so my ring remains buried forever. After that, I always put it in my pocket for safety, most especially when I was gardening.

I wanted to have a proper reception for the guests at my wedding and asked the local baker in Seaview, "Would you be able to do a nice reception for me? I know that rationing might make it difficult but what are the possibilities?" He said, "As you are getting married in June I could do you

Margaret and Leonard on their wedding day in June 1942. Margaret's dress was pink and the other Wrens formed a guard of honour as she came out of the church in Seaview.

a nice salad as we can grow that. We can also have home grown potatoes and have half a pound of cheese, your ration allowance for one week." All this had to stretch to 33 guests and surprisingly it did!

The wedding breakfast cost 3 shillings and 6 pence per head. My mother and father had to apply for travel permits to come to the Island for the wedding. They travelled by paddle steamer and had to go back to Southampton on the one designated to them by the authorities.

Due to very stringent rationing during the war we were unable to use sugar to make icing for the wedding cake and the baker had to be very innovative. He made marzipan with a type of semolina to get a nice white colouring which looked as close to icing as he could get. He then added some almond essence, covered the outside with rice paper carefully and in the joins of the rice paper added layers of artificial flowers. It was very difficult to get hold of any dried fruit for the cake mix but as usual everyone rallied round and one Wren was able to offer one half pound of prunes. The baker cut them up very carefully and made them into currant shapes and together with another Wren's offering of a quarter pound of raisins a very nice and tasty wedding cake was made. He then put the pink artificial roses around the cake and it looked very beautiful.

I wore a pink wedding dress, which had been a dress I had worn as a bridesmaid, and had a borrowed veil. I was unable to get a white dress due to strict rationing.

Make do and mend was very much the order of the day during the war but it made us very creative and we found new and different ways to do things. We were not really, at least most of the time, unhappy with our lot. We had a very important job to do and we did it to the best of our ability. Many did it by sacrificing their lives for others.

I was married in the Methodist Church in Seaview and after the lovely service I came out of the church with my husband, Leonard. He was 28 years old. There was a guard of honour by my fellow Wrens. In the photograph, as I was coming out of the church and through my arch of Wrens, there laid carefully in the corner was my gas mask. It still makes me laugh today to think about it but as Service personnel we had to wear special gas masks that were rather more complicated than the ordinary issue. We had to be able to walk around whilst wearing it and keep on going and do whatever needed

Margaret and Leonard setting off on their honeymoon to the New Forest for a much deserved holiday.

to be done during an air raid. It was a vital part of our duties.

There is a lovely, funny photograph of myself and my fellow Wrens on a gas training course in Portsmouth. We were there to learn how to use our masks properly. In one of the photographs we are all posed, in naval uniform and with our faces completely covered with the gas masks. It was not a glamorous look, indeed we looked like something out of a science-fiction story. The training itself was quite frightening. We had to go through the Tipnor Gas Tank, remove our gas masks and rush quickly to the exit. The smell was awful and we emerged with streaming eyes and lots of coughing and spluttering. The thought of being in a gas attack was very frightening and it brought home the reality of how dangerous and unpleasant that would be.

Leonard, my lovely husband and I honeymooned in the New Forest. We only had two days there before he received a telegram informing him that his father had died. Sadly, our honeymoon was over early.

Everyone travelling to and from the Isle of Wight had to have a special permit during the war so travel backwards

On a gas training course in Portsmouth pictured with our gas masks on at the top. Not a glamorous look! and below, without the masks, So much prettier! Margaret is third from left on the top row pictured with other Wrens.

16

and forwards to the mainland was very difficult. As the Island was considered a very strategic and important spot it had to be protected from German invasion. The permit had to state how much time you were spending there and the reasons for your visit. It was very strictly adhered to and of course we all understood why.

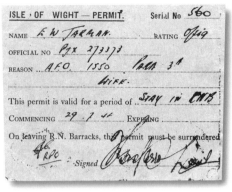

A travel permit was required to travel to and from the Isle of Wight.

The proximity to Portsmouth where so many Naval ships were moored made it imperative that the Island did not have infiltrators sympathetic to the German war effort. The ships themselves were an obvious target for the Luftwaffe.

The restrictions were also applied to near relatives of Island dwellers as I have already mentioned. The permit itself was very difficult to obtain and there had to be very good reasons for the trip. The local newspaper, the Isle of Wight County Press, at the time described it as a 'Necessary but most inconvenient isolation' The County Press is still the Island's newspaper and is as informative today as it was during those war years. Some things don't change, fortunately.

Although travel on and off the Island was difficult we did manage to do so on occasions. As my family lived on the mainland I was granted permission to travel to Fair Oak in Eastleigh where they lived. My father had been the Chief Engineer on private yachts before the war. Perhaps that is why I so wanted to join the Wrens and follow in my father's footsteps.

*Examples of German propaganda
leaflets dropped from their aircraft. One picture shows a
British prisoner of war imprisoned in a German prison camp.*

On one occasion I had visited my parents in Eastleigh. It was Double Summertime, two hours forward instead of one from Greenwich Mean Time (GMT). This was, of course, to save electricity and keep industry and farming working as efficiently as possible.

I would normally have left my parents at 3 o'clock in the afternoon but father had suggested I stay longer as it was now much lighter into the evening. I was happy to have a few more hours with my family as I did not get to see them that often. When I eventually got to Portsmouth Harbour the train I should have been on had been completely destroyed. It had been bombed by the Germans. Travelling later had saved my life, yet another escape from either death or very nasty injuries.

As I mentioned earlier people formed all kinds of friendships during the war and some were in very strange circumstances indeed.

It was a common occurrence, at that time, for the Germans to drop propaganda leaflets in order to undermine the war effort and to make people feel that we were losing the war and would eventually be ruled by them.

My sister, Patricia had such a leaflet, which had fallen in the back garden from one of these air drops. She was looking at it as she sat down on the bus to travel home one day. The leaflet had been found near Winchester. She had sat next to a distressed woman who had not heard from her son in a very long time.

As they both looked at the pictures on the leaflet the woman suddenly cried, "That's my son there." It later turned out that he was a prisoner of war in Germany and at the end of the war he came home safely.

This was a most amazing coincidence and an outcome that the Germans had not intended, to comfort someone who believed she had lost her beloved son.

It was not the only coincidence of it's kind. A photograph of a gravestone in a Commonwealth War Cemetery had been taken by a visitor to the graveyard. The gravestone belonged to a young man, only 18, who had been killed in the Normandy landings in 1944. He came from Bembridge on the Isle of Wight and had served with the Hampshire Regiment. By chance the photograph was shown to a friend of the family and eventually the family were shown the picture. Later his two brothers visited the grave. They had never known previously what had happened to him.

CHAPTER FOUR

Culver Signal Station

As mentioned earlier Culver Cliffs in Bembridge was home to the Wrens who were the Wireless Operators. The buildings they were housed in were the old Coast Guard cottages. It was a very windy and isolated place to be. Later on these cottages became private dwellings.

Fort Bembridge, where the wireless room was located, was about a mile away from their living quarters. The Culver Signal Station, now an inn, was the only wireless station which picked up distress signals from the submarine *MS Thetis* which tragically sank in Liverpool Bay in the 1930's.

I went every other week with the Chief Writer Pay, as I was then a Leading Wren, to give the Wrens their pay. It was a formal affair but much less so than at Puckpool. They received their money in a rather nice sitting room.

Culver was an area which could not be easily accessed by civilians as it was such an obvious target for the Germans. Security tended to be tight and people were turned away unless they had a valid reason to be there.

My husband's band used to play at Culver and once as they were going up on to the cliffs they noticed that a low flying German plane seemed to be surveying the area and that there appeared to be one light flashing from the Lake area.

Coincidentally one particular woman kept on being found on the Culver Down. Although she was not supposed to be there she always had an excuse, usually that her dog had run away and

Culver Down, Bembridge. Concrete fortifications and gun emplacements remaining from the Second World War.

she was searching for him. Investigations found that her house was the one in Lake with the light on and it was subsequently discovered that she was signalling to the Germans.

Her name was Dorothy O'Grady. She was arrested and charged under the Treachery Act for the offences which had taken place on the Isle of Wight. Her trial took place at Winchester Crown Court and she was found guilty and sentenced to death.

Later at the Court of Appeal her sentence was transmuted to 14 years imprisonment. Lord Chief Justice, Lord Caldecot gave his decision in private although he had allowed Mrs O'Grady's husband, a postman, to be present in court to hear the arguments before the final decision was made. Mrs O'Grady served her 14 years and was then released.

It turned out later that Mrs O'Grady was part of a spy ring of three people. One was based in Brighton and the other in Bournemouth.

After serving 18 months at *HMS Medina*, I was transferred to *HMS Osborne* which was based at the Pier Hotel in Seaview. The pay centre was at the Esplanade Hotel and was on the corner of George Street and the Esplanade in Ryde. I travelled to Ryde every day to do my job and reported in occasionally to headquarters in Seaview. There were no Fleet Air Arm Personnel based in Ryde but there were plenty of sailors scattered around the area.

The other Wrens on the Island were often the oldest child in their families. In those days most of the Wrens had left boyfriends at home and they did not often have affairs. They also tended to marry younger than many women do today.

Although we worked hard there was some time to have fun and make friends. One of my friends, a fellow Wren, was Elsie.

HMS Warspite was anchored at Ryde Pier towards the end of the war. The Wrens had been invited on board for tea with the sailors. The ship had a long, steep ladder and Elsie was the last Wren to clamber up before the sailors began their ascent. She appeared to be having a little trouble climbing up and was rather slow.

One of the sailors was clearly getting rather impatient with her seemingly slow progress and he called out, "For god's sake woman get a move on. What do you think they issued you with those elasticated knickers for?"

Poor Elsie was absolutely mortified. She was quite a sedate lady and was not at all amused with what she viewed as a very uncouth outburst on his part.

Eventually she was transferred to *HMS Vernon* in Portsmouth, another land based unit. On the Island, at Medina, she had worked in the police office on the gate.

The Esplanade Hotel, Ryde. During the war it was the Navy's Pay Centre.

Being new to Portsmouth, when Elsie went to have her first bath there she found it so extremely dirty, which did not meet with her high standards, that she went to find some Vim to scour it clean. After thoroughly cleaning the bath she took back the Vim and upon returning she found it occupied by another Wren who exclaimed "Some idiot has cleaned the bath so I'm just enjoying it!"

Poor Elsie, caught out because she insisted on being so fastidious and correct in taking back the cleaning materials to the kitchen some considerable distance away!

CHAPTER FIVE

Make do and Mend

Make do and mend was definitely the order of the day in wartime. It was a necessity so whether we liked it or not, we had to just get on with it. That was true in all aspects of life that we take so much for granted today. Whether it was to do with food or clothing, because of rationing, we all had to learn to be both innovative and creative. And this we certainly did. Very little was wasted.

The government of the day issued booklets containing advice and menus to make the most of the foods we were able to obtain. Because of rationing food was so scarce and many ingredients for meals were simply not available.

Just to illustrate how difficult it was and how excited we were when we did get food treats, I remember vividly being on a train travelling to my parents home in Eastleigh in Hampshire chatting to a very kind young sailor. In fact he was so kind he actually gave me a banana. I had not even seen one of those for an absolute age and it was such a treat.

Being one of six children, me being the eldest, I did not eat the banana but took it home to share with them. Even though it had been divided into so many pieces it was absolutely mouth-wateringly delicious. We could not believe how excited we could get over one banana! In many ways food never tasted so good as then, perhaps because we had those kinds of treats so rarely.

One of the books written for the times was called 'Good Eating' and published for the Daily Telegraph. The little

The Ministry of Information's 'Make Do and Mend'. One of the many booklets issued to advise on cheap meals and clothing.

book was two shillings, in pre-decimalisation currency. The book was mainly full of recipes sent in by readers. In many ways it was a forerunner of the way people now experiment with food and make up new dishes. Wartime rationing certainly focussed minds on how to get the best taste out of food, Before the war herbs were not used so much in food but with the necessity that people had to use cheaper cuts of meat then experimentation with different herbs was probably inevitable. The restriction was limited to a monetary amount, in those days 1 shilling and 2 pence. Today the equivalent of less than 7 pence. This meant that we had to choose between quantity or quality of meat. Quantity often won especially if there were many mouths to feed. Rabbit was always a great favourite.

I have always been interested in cooking so tried a number of the recipes published in this book. One of the most

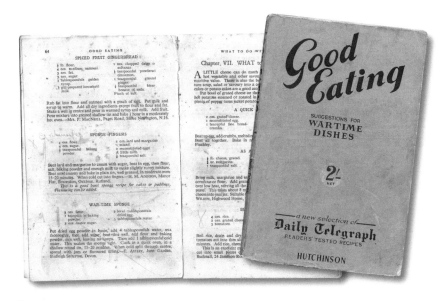

'Good Eating' containing Margaret's favourite 'Wartime Sponge' pudding recipe.

interesting things about the recipes are the small quantities of food required, very important in wartime.

Inevitably at this time too, cheaper cuts of meat became popular, a necessity because of the stringent rationing policy in place. It had been traditional to use the meats available for roasting but as the supply diminished meats for stewing had to be used. Housewives were amazed at how tasty they were even though they had to be cooked more slowly and for longer. During the war nothing could be wasted and braising, boiling and pot roasting was necessary in order to cook these cheaper joints so as to enjoy their flavour fully. Marinading too was a practise adopted by the housewives for tougher joints. This added flavour to the meat. As I reflect back and examine this little book today, I note my comments as to whether I found the recipe successful or not.

One of my favourites was called 'war time sponge' and was made with little more than some flour, some baking powder, caster sugar, dried egg and water. It only took about 15 to 20 minutes to cook in the oven, so did not use up much electricity, and could be split down the centre so that you could just add some jam or another kind of flavoured sweet filling. It was very tasty and altogether a very economical dish.

Another of the recipes was related to cheese. Apparently the chef of a large peacetime luxury liner took charge of one of the war canteens and tried to introduce cheese recipes that were more tasty. Many of the women war workers who made munitions used the canteen. After a long hard day they were usually served bread, cheese and salads. They were often very tired and mostly left their cheese portion as it was so hard to digest. They were really ready to flop into their beds after their long working hours.

The chef decided to put the cheese through a mincer and pressed it into small round pots. He then turned them out as baby cheeses. He finished them off by carving a nice criss-cross pattern into the tops and served them on a bed of lettuce.

The women found them so much more appetising and from then on there were no more cheese left overs. A good example then of how much difference food looking good makes and also by breaking down the hardness of the cheese made them so much more digestible.

The ration for cheese was two ounces per week and this meant that recipes needed to be nourishing to take advantage of the nutritional value and all the protein and goodness that it contained. It was a bit tough if you did not like cheese.

However if you did not there was always that old favourite the dried egg. Fresh eggs were indeed very difficult to obtain in war time so dried eggs were mainly used. There was very lively debate as to the pros and cons of whether to reconstitute the eggs (by adding water or milk if you could get) or simply use it in its dried form. Some considered that mixing dried egg directly into the cake mix made for much lighter cakes.

During wartime, of course, there was great encouragement to grow our own food. Plenty of fruit was grown though according to season and depending on their natural growth time. That meant there were plenty of apples and pears and prunes in winter and rhubarb in the spring and of course many of the soft fruits such as blackberries in the summer.

One of the book's recipes was an all year round table jelly using whichever fruit was available according to the time of year.

We were also encouraged to make 'apple butter' a very popular choice in America. This was achieved by cooking apples slowly until tender, mixing the pulp with sugar and cooking until very thick and smooth. Potting it in small jars meant that it could be used up quickly as it did not have a very long shelf life.

As I look back over those years, I realise just how hard it was for families, with the men away fighting and the women having to be deployed into the munitions factories and the farms where many became the land army, as they were called. They learned how to grow and harvest the food that the nation was so badly in need of and did a tremendously important job as they took the place of the men away fighting the war. In fact, they transformed home cookery.

CHAPTER SIX

Wartime Luxuries

As I have indicated on a number of occasions, wartime was not a time for luxuries but in many ways we had to develop our creative skills. There is no doubt that rationing encouraged us all to think about how we could achieve our aims.

My sister Pamela's wedding was such an example. Her husband was in the army in North Africa, the 8th Army under Montgomery. He eventually got to Northern Italy and was then selected to come home to collect an award which had been given to General Montgomery. He was happy to do this so he could get married.

The wedding reception was held at Johnny's Duver Club in Seaview. There were not enough coupons to buy a wedding dress so my sister had to borrow one. Coupons were not required for muslin material so my sister purchased 30 yards of butter muslin. The coupons were then used to buy four nightdresses in a very pretty blue and the dressmaker made four muslin dresses to go over them. The gorgeous, diaphanous quality of the muslin allowed the blue of the nightdresses to shine through beautifully. So pretty were they that the young bridesmaids did not want to part with their dresses after the wedding ceremony.

Eventually they were persuaded that if they did not then the bride would not have a nightdress to wear on her honeymoon. Reluctantly, two of them parted with them after much persuasion.

It was rare during the war for girls to get a new dress let alone such a pretty one. Materials such as curtain material or old

Clothing coupons, without which clothes could not be purchased and a pair of silk stockings as worn by the Officers during the Second World war. These are still in pristine, unworn condition.

satin bedding material were often used when necessary for special celebrations.

Another way of developing our creative skills was to learn how to carry out a light degree of smuggling. As you might imagine women were treated very differently from the men. One example of this was regarding the purchase of tobacco. Only the men were allowed to purchase it from the stores. The cost was one and tuppence (twopence) for a half-pound tin of tobacco and one shilling and one penny for a packet of cigarettes. At my Medina posting those women who wished to buy tobacco had to ask the other men to get it for them. I did not smoke but as my husband smoked a pipe I wanted to be able to get him some pipe tobacco.

The men were happy to purchase the tobacco on our behalves but once we had got it we had to find a way to smuggle it out of camp. We decided to use marrows and very carefully cut out the middle of the vegetable so the tobacco could be hidden inside. The marrows were grown by the gardener who was employed to cut the grass. He sold them to us for two pence. When we smuggled out the tobacco the marrows sat very carefully in the baskets with only the top third of them showing. At first we were very anxious about this practice but soon got used to the idea when we were not challenged. Even though I was not a smoker myself it was nice to be able to give my husband a present that he enjoyed at that time.

Some of the funny postcards of the time. Humour was still evident. These were sent to Margaret by her husband.

CHAPTER SEVEN

HMS Osborne

As the war progressed our lovely island saw a lot of movement in the war effort and there were a number of bizarre casualties too.

The Seaview Suspension Pier, a quite fragile structure but unique and beautiful, which was eventually washed away in the 1950's, had been instrumental in getting the Air and Sea Rescue in and out of the Island. Close by was the Pier Hotel, it was taken over by the Navy and used as a sick bay for naval personnel. Sadly the building is no longer there. This was *HMS Osborne* where I was later stationed in 1942.

A boom had been erected between the Duver at Seaview and Southsea, on the mainland. This was to protect the harbour from infiltration from German submarines. There was however, a small area for our own vessels to manoeuvre in and out again. The gap was protected by small vessels on each side of it. These each had a small complement of men on board at all times.

One day I was on duty and giving out pay when a man in a wheelchair came in to collect his wages. After he had left the office I asked the Petty Officer about him and he told me the most amazing story.

This very brave man was in charge of guarding the gap when a terrific storm blew up. The weather was so bad that his vessel had rocketed against the barricade causing the ship to break up. All the men were thrown into the water. He managed to grab the rope and tied each man to it. One man had lost his rope so this Officer took off his own and tied it

A pre-First War postcard showing the Seaview Suspension Pier, now lost after a storm in the 1950s.

to his subordinate. He himself then clung onto the tramline barriers with his bare hands. All the men were saved but he himself suffered severe damage to his legs and was rescued by the Bembridge Lifeboat.

Just after the war had ended, I saw him again. I had taken a job in the New Forest where I then lived. The man came in to buy seed boxes. I thought he looked familiar, although miraculously he was now walking. He had regained the use of his legs.

His hands were very scarred because he had had to cling on for so long once he had given up his own rope. He had, as a result, severely damaged his hands.

Many years later I was listening to the BBC when the coxswain of the Bembridge Lifeboat was being interviewed. He then told the above story. He had also asked for memories of listeners and after the programme I had telephoned him. He was very interested to meet and share more reminisces but sadly died before we could meet.

He did share one other thing however as we talked on the phone. He had been on holiday in the Orkneys and actually met the same man. He was now in charge of a ferry boat in the Shetlands.

What a hero that man was and what a wonderful story of the human spirit. He never gave up and overcame his injuries to go on to lead a fulfilling life doing what he loved to do. The war produced many such people.

CHAPTER EIGHT

Precautions

When I was off duty air raids were often spent with granny sitting in the dining room with our steel helmets on. This protected us against any shrapnel which may have been flying about if we were hit by the bombs. The air raids could last anything from thirty minutes to an hour and as you can imagine a lot of time was wasted in this way.

I have already mentioned about the steel table which we sat under in air raids to protect ourselves from the bombs. This had been provided by the ARP (Air Raid Precautions). Many civilians were a part of this invaluable team of people. They did just about everything from giving advice on sensible precautions to take during air raids to ensuring that the whole community knew what was happening. For example what to do when bombs had fallen on houses and streets. It was important for people to keep as safe as possible and to be informed of anything particularly dangerous.

ARP always inspected at blackout, to ensure that no German bomber planes could see their targets. Every household was required to maintain the blackout code and not show any glimpses of light to the outside world. The ARP walked around every night in order to keep the Isle of Wight as safe as it could be. It was a dangerous place to live given it's geographical importance. ARP volunteers were amongst many of the unsung heroes of the Second World War

I still have a little booklet, an album of cigarette cards issued by W.D & H.O. Wills, a branch of the Imperial Tobacco Company.

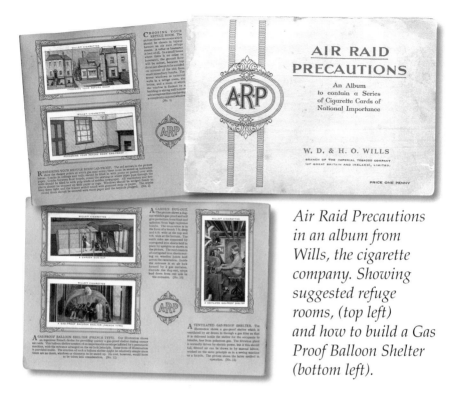

Air Raid Precautions in an album from Wills, the cigarette company. Showing suggested refuge rooms, (top left) and how to build a Gas Proof Balloon Shelter (bottom left).

The cover described the cards as 'Cigarette Cards of National Importance' And so they were. The booklet was priced one penny, pre-decimalisation rate.

The booklet was endorsed by Samuel Hoare, the then Home Secretary who provided the foreword to the publication.

He particularly highlighted that many of the precautions could be implemented for very little cost and even the more expensive ones could be in collaboration with friends and neighbours. He wrote that they were commonsense suggestions and demanded "Ingenuity and improvisation rather than expenditure." He finished his foreword by writing "I commend a study of these cards to your attention."

Each cigarette card also had a narrative showing how to actually achieve the end result. For example 'Choosing your refuge room' went through all the possible options and even went on to inform as to items that should be contained in this room. Many people used their cellars as their refuge if they had one.

One of the problems during this time was the possibility of being poisoned by gas, so much emphasis was placed on how to avoid this, from the use of gas masks to how to make a door gas proof.

One of the illustrations is of a 'Gas Proof Balloon Shelter (French Type).' It consists of an impermeable envelope inflated by a pneumatic machine with the entrance arranged on an air lock principle. It had no windows or doors and was described as being relatively simple because of this fact. It did caution however, that the cost would have to be considered.

Interestingly the booklet contains a lot of pictures of women for example, using fire pumps and even how to carry an incendiary bomb out of the house. Women of course, at this time were having major life changes and having to become the head of the household whilst men were away fighting the war.

As young women in wartime we were unworried. Crime levels on the Island were not at all high and everyone pulled together more. The enemy were Germans not each other.

In the black out, we liked it when the moon was shining but that of course made it easier for the Germans to bomb their targets more accurately.

Of course in those days it was easier to travel too as the trains ran right around the Island.

CHAPTER NINE

A Second Front

There had been a number of indications that the Second Front was imminent. We had noticed that a huge number of boats, vessels and crafts of all kind were moored in the Solent, at Spithead, between Portsmouth and Ryde. I remember thinking that there were so many lined up one behind another that if I wanted to I could probably walk from Portsmouth to Ryde just by climbing from one boat to another.

Another very telling clue was the fact that we had been instructed to pay the men three weeks money. We normally only had to pay them every two weeks. It was very clear to us that something was about to happen.

A number of Thames Lighterman also arrived on the Island and marching at the helm with them was no less a figure than Lord Louis Mountbatten. As they marched on parade with their very non-naval clothing they would greet everyone with a very cockney "Hiya mate." They were on the Island to instruct the Naval personnel in the best use of the barges, many of which had been conscripted for the exercise. The leader of the men in this brigade of London bargemen was Dod Osborne, a very eccentric character who was well known for his daredevil exploits, particularly for sailing a fishing boat across the Atlantic. He was a very interesting man and had an outgoing and inspirational way about him.

The fishing boat was the *Girl Pat*. It was rumoured that he had stolen it but after the war it was reported that he was on a secret mission and the craft had been fitted with sophisticated

I feel I cannot let you leave 21 Army Group on your return to civil life without a message of thanks and farewell. Together we have carried through one of the most successful campaigns in history, and it has been our good fortune to be members of this great team. God Bless you and God speed.

B. L. Montgomery

FIELD MARSHAL
COMMANDER IN CHIEF

BLA ·1945

A copy of the letter sent out to Margaret's husband, Leonard Munday at the end of the war. Written by Montgomery to service personnel thanking them for the brave contribution they made to the war effort.

navigational equipment in order to be able to get important information about enemy submarines and how the Navy could avoid them in the waters off the coast of Portugal. There was always a lot of speculation about the true facts surrounding the mystery of what happened to the *Girl Pat*.

The war continued sadly to take casualties, many of whom died. On a small island like this it was inevitable that we knew many of them quite well. We had either gone to school with them or grown up together. Amongst these losses were young men of my age. One died as a rear-gunner in a plane, another on a battleship which had been sunk off the coast of Scotland.

But for all of the sad and tragic happenings there were many lighter moments, even very funny ones. My sister-in-law, her husband and daughter lived next to her mother-in-law, in Southampton. Both houses were bombed out so they looked for new homes and found two cottages, next door to each other. One day my sister-in-law was in the outside lavatory, which had wooden walls, when an air raid started.

As she sat on the toilet a brass shell came hurtling through the roof. It frightened the life out of her but amazingly fell straight between her legs and did not explode. She never moved so quickly.

Later on the brass shell was kept as an ornament on her mantelpiece. A memento of that lucky moment perhaps. It was soon moved however when they were told that it could still explode. They felt their luck had been tested enough.

German Occupation Money given to the troops after the war. This might have been similar to how our currency would have looked if the Germans had won.

CHAPTER TEN

Brading

Margaret continues to live on the Isle of Wight in Brading where she started the Antique Toy Museum in Brading which has featured on the BBC a number of times because of it's old and interesting collection. Her son, Graham and his wife Jacqueline, run it now.

I think this following story sums up the tenacious spirit that Margaret has. Her daughter, Katherine, then about ten years of age, had started to collect dolls dressed in national costume but did not have a Russian one. The family wrote to President Krushchev and after some months, to their surprise,

a doll arrived. The story, not surprisingly, made the national headlines.

Margaret has attended many reunions with other Wrens and ex-servicemen since those war years including a fiftieth anniversary in 1994 which featured in the Isle of Wight County Press. She

Dolls given as thanks for being rescued.
Donated to the Doll's Museum by prisoners of war.

has amazing energy and continues to give talks about her experiences as a Wren and about the Toy Museum.

As Margaret relayed her wartime experiences to me she stressed that she had not done anything amazing, or indeed special, but without that strength of spirit that she, and so many others, displayed at that time and at such a young age, the outcome could have been very different. The German money given to troops occupying Germany at the end of the war may have become the currency of our country.

I write Margaret's experiences as a tribute to her and to all her fellow Wrens who did such an amazing job of work during the war and to all the women who took up the challenge and rose to it with dignity and courage.

Fifty years on in June 1994. With Margaret are two Culver Signallers, Edna Dodds (left) and Enid Nelson-Ward (right). Enid is a descendant of Lord Nelson. How appropriate for a Wren!

42

Memories of an Ordinary WREN
Margaret Munday-Whitaker

Chamberlain said "We are at war" and Hitler we must stay.
It's now too late for peace treaties, there seems no other way"
So be prepared all you young men, and girls we'll also need
And slightly older ones as well and some will have to lead.

Fathers, Uncles, Brothers too, all joined up their bit to do
We joined the WRENS, and gave our best. It certainly put us to the test,
To release the men, we'd come to stay, enabling them to get away
To get away and serve at sea where, after all, they'd rather be.

Cyphers, writers, W.T, stokers, stores, and cooks were we.
We manned the 'phones both night and day and oh! for so little pay.
Despatch Riders, they roared around, on bikes as large as could be found.
In blackout conditions, with often bombs falling.
They couldn't afford to find their bikes stalling.
In ice and snow and pouring rain, never once did they complain.
We took on the lot, so the men could be free,
What a versatile bunch were we!

We learned new words like Quarter Deck, Divisions, Oppo,
Hook Gannet, Galley, Cabins and SA 43 Pay Book.
We didn't want our friends to go but, when promoted it had to be so.
And we felt quite sad when pals get drafts,
so we had a party - full of laughs.
We promised we'd meet again one day.
"Under the clock at Waterloo" we'd say.

Photos were taken - some still survive,
We'd like to think they're still alive.
But where they're not, we think of them still,
Their presence is with us - always will.

Then in 45, "It's Over!" they said, so our uniforms we began to shed,
Fiancées to marry, or husbands to join,
Homes to be found and new lives to plan.
Families to raise, new friends to be made,
our days in the WRENS began to fade.

Later our children said, "Mum don't keep on so,
That's history, it happened so long ago,"
But to us and our comrades it meant such a lot, in good days and bad
We had cared for each other,
They'll never know, what it meant to their Mother.

Then in nineteen hundred and seventy three,
An association was forming, we heard with much glee.
The news went around "we really must go,
With a great deal of luck, might meet someone we know"
And even if not, it doesn't matter,
We've made new friends and have a good natter.

We talk of the past, and future as well,
For a couple of hours, we're under the spell.
Our days in the WRENS and all that it meant,
An hour or two really very well spent.

And so we've arrived at '98, our silver Anniversary to celebrate,
With Connie and Hilda and Helen too,
Without Barbara and Officers, What would we do?
The committee works hard and we thank them all,
And say "Long live our Association, may it never fail"

Acknowledgements

My grateful thanks go to Margaret Munday-Whitaker who helped to make this book possible.
Thanks to the Wight Fair Writers Group for their encouragement and insightful comments.
Ken Wheeler at Pressready Artwork for layout and photography.

Photograph Credits:
Margaret Munday-Whitaker's own collection:
page 2, 6, 9, 11, 13, 15, 16, 17, 18, 25, 26, 30, 31, 33, 36, 39, 40, 41.
K. Wheeler: page 21, 23.
M. North: page 4.
Isle of Wight County Press: page 42.

Cover Design: K. Wheeler.